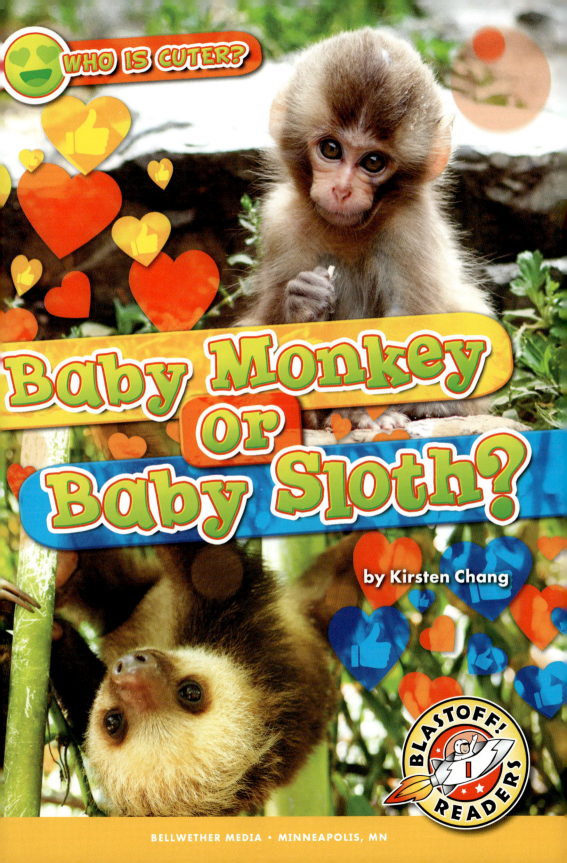

Blastoff! Readers are carefully developed by literacy experts to build reading stamina and move students toward fluency by combining standards-based content with developmentally appropriate text.

Level 1 provides the most support through repetition of high-frequency words, light text, predictable sentence patterns, and strong visual support.

Level 2 offers early readers a bit more challenge through varied sentences, increased text load, and text-supportive special features.

Level 3 advances early-fluent readers toward fluency through increased text load, less reliance on photos, advancing concepts, longer sentences, and more complex special features.

★ **Blastoff! Universe**

Reading Level

Grade K · Grades 1–3 · Grade 4

This edition first published in 2026 by Bellwether Media, Inc.

No part of this publication may be reproduced in whole or in part without written permission of the publisher. For information regarding permission, write to Bellwether Media, Inc., Attention: Permissions Department, 6012 Blue Circle Drive, Minnetonka, MN 55343.

Library of Congress Cataloging-in-Publication Data

Names: Chang, Kirsten, 1991- author
Title: Baby monkey or baby sloth? / by Kirsten Chang.
Description: Minneapolis, MN : Bellwether Media, Inc, 2026. | Series: Blastoff! Readers: Who Is cuter? | Includes bibliographical references and index. | Audience: Ages 5-8 | Audience: Grades K-1 | Summary: "Developed by literacy experts for students in kindergarten through grade three, this book introduces baby monkeys and baby sloths to young readers through leveled text and related photos"– Provided by publisher.
Identifiers: LCCN 2025003203 (print) | LCCN 2025003204 (ebook) | ISBN 9798893044461 library binding | ISBN 9798893045840 ebook
Subjects: LCSH: Monkeys–Infancy | Sloths–Infancy
Classification: LCC QL737.P9 C455 2026 (print) | LCC QL737.P9 (ebook) | DDC 599.813/92-dc23/eng/20250317
LC record available at https://lccn.loc.gov/2025003203
LC ebook record available at https://lccn.loc.gov/2025003204

Text copyright © 2026 by Bellwether Media, Inc. BLASTOFF! READERS and associated logos are trademarks and/or registered trademarks of Bellwether Media, Inc. Bellwether Media is a division of FlutterBee Education Group.

Editor: Rachael Barnes   Designer: Brittany McIntosh

Printed in the United States of America, North Mankato, MN.

Table of Contents

Infants and Babies	4
Fur and Tails	8
Fast and Slow	14
Who Is Cuter?	20
Glossary	22
To Learn More	23
Index	24

Infants and Babies

Baby monkeys are called infants. Baby sloths are simply called babies.

baby

infant

These **mammals** are cute! They both stay close to mom.

Fur and Tails

Both mammals are born with fur. Infant fur may change color. Baby fur gets **coarse**.

coarse fur

Infants have fingers and toes. Babies have long **claws**.

Nearly all infants have tails. Some use their tails to swing! Few babies have tails.

tail →

Fast and Slow

Older infants are fast!
They run and play.
Babies are slow.
They sleep a lot!

15

Older infants eat fruit, seeds, and bugs. Babies eat leaves.

Infants often hold onto mom's back. Babies **cling** to mom's chest. Which is cuter?

clinging to mom

Who Is Cuter?

different colors of fur

tail

fingers and toes

Baby Monkey

runs and plays

eats fruit, seeds, and bugs

holds onto mom's back

Glossary

claws

sharp, curved nails

mammals

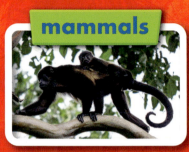

warm-blooded animals that have backbones and feed their young milk

cling

to hold onto tightly

coarse

rough

To Learn More

AT THE LIBRARY

Brandle, Marie. *Monkey Infants in the Wild*. Minneapolis, Minn.: Jump!, 2023.

Gish, Melissa. *Sloths*. Mankato, Minn.: Creative Education and Creative Paperbacks, 2024.

Nilsen, Genevieve. *Sloth Babies*. Minneapolis, Minn.: Jump!, 2021.

ON THE WEB

FACTSURFER

Factsurfer.com gives you a safe, fun way to find more information.

1. Go to www.factsurfer.com.

2. Enter "baby monkey or baby sloth" into the search box and click 🔍.

3. Select your book cover to see a list of related content.

Index

bugs, 16
claws, 10, 11
cling, 18, 19
color, 8
eat, 16
fingers, 10, 11
fruit, 16
fur, 8, 9
leaves, 16
mammals, 6, 8
mom, 6, 18, 19
monkeys, 4
play, 14
run, 14
seeds, 16

sleep, 14
sloths, 4
swing, 12
tails, 12, 13
toes, 10

The images in this book are reproduced through the courtesy of: L-N, front cover (monkey); Kristel Segeren, front cover (sloth), p. 21 (bottom left, bottom right); Eric Isselee, pp. 3 (top, bottom), 20 (main), 21 (main); Matthew W Keefe, p. 5 (sloth); achikochi, p. 5 (monkey); Yangguza, p. 7 (monkey); Nature Picture Library/ Alamy, p. 7 (sloth); Urs Hauenstein/ Alamy, pp. 9 (sloth), 19 (sloth); Katsiaryna Shchuchkina, p. 9 (monkey); Suzi Eszterhas, p. 11 (sloth); S. Hatsumori, p. 11 (monkey); Rosanne Tackaberry/ Alamy, p. 13 (sloth); worldswildlifewonders, p. 13 (monkey); Víctor Santamaría González/ Alamy, p. 15 (sloth); salajean, p. 15 (monkey); trubavin, p. 17 (monkey); Dean Bouton, p. 17 (sloth); Eric Gevaert, p. 19 (monkey); Sompao, p. 20 (bottom left); jurra8, p. 20 (bottom center); Anna Kucherova, p. 20 (bottom right); Damocean/ Getty Images, p. 21 (bottom center); Mark_Kostich, p. 22 (claws); Manamana, p. 22 (cling); Wondry, p. 22 (coarse); Wollertz, p. 22 (mammals).